NOTES ON VANISHING

NOTES ON VANISHING

poems by

Cammy Pedroja

Cider Press Review
San Diego

Cider Press Review
PO BOX 33384
San Diego, CA, USA
CIDERPRESSREVIEW.COM

First edition
10 9 8 7 6 5 4 3 2 1 0

ISBN: 9781930781566
Library of Congress Control Number: 2020930519
CoverArt: Edvard Munch, Two Women on the Shore, 1898,
    The Art Institute of Chicago.
Author photograph by Angel Gill
Book design by Caron Andregg

Winner of the 2018 *Cider Press Review* Book Award:
CIDERPRESSREVIEW.COM/BOOKAWARD.

Printed in the United States of America
at Bookmobile in Minneapolis, MN USA.

For Ben, Lottie, and Jane.
For Andi, Annika, Ella, Fran, and Liza.
For anyone telling the truth after a long silence.

ACKNOWLEDGMENTS

Thank you to the editors of the following publications, in which these poems have appeared:

"Bones and Light" (published as "Bone Poem"), *FIELD*
"Into the Deeps," *New England Review*
"Ants Eating Poison," *Mid-American Review* (winner of the 2018 James
    Wright Poetry Prize)
"Island View," *Western Humanities Review*
"Adulation in a Storm" (published as "Notes on Vanishing"), *PANK*
"Shedding," *PANK*
"On the Land," *Little Jackie Paper*
"A Last Note," *Verse Daily*
"Exposure," *Bacon Review*
"A New Language," *Bacon Review*
"The Invisible Man," *Ragazine*
"Question," *Ragazine*
"Time Travel," *Ragazine*

TABLE OF CONTENTS

…we disappear.

It happens to me frequently. You disappear? Yes and then come back.

Moments of death I call them.

— Anne Carson, *Autobiography of Red*

I. Earth

MOUNTAIN PEOPLE LAMENT

I can clean and trim the hoof
of a goat with its neck locked
between boards of a sty.

The Mother taught me
to close my mouth and hide
behind the tin shed
when a car passed by.

Illness is the author of it and I,
the pitted fruit
fallen from the tree   dissolving.

I come from a long line of unschooled women.

Pale and translucent,
crooked bite of bobcats.

I'm part of a long line of children
to whom I must pay penance
for deserting, abandoning, railing
against the way I felt their histories ensnare me.

I'm sorry I left you. I'm sorry I left you.
How could I have left you there, still walking
up and down the road, waiting
for the mountain line bus to rattle by?

Some hilltop Spirit carries my burdens
around with her—
they jingle in her pocket like keys.

TIME TRAVEL

Every day I am young again
in a fouled brown house
on the Mountain.

Malevolent weeds erupt
upward like cold sores
on the landscape.

I see myself, arms with claw marks,
a group of scabbed white cats
huddling around the screen door
to get in.

I want to empty the acreage
of specters, fall out of touch with
its secrets.

Cutting through the underbrush

warning bangs
the inside of my chest—
I am carrying my recollection.
Getting her out of there.

BONES AND LIGHT

You look abstract, like a bridesmaid

and groom your hair as though measuring out

yards of brown silk.

I *do* forget (against the bust of you)

that we are only so many feet

from a road　　　　　also nettles grow,

Provenance hides in the trees,

but look how far your arm bends

around my stem

as I lie down in the grass like an artifact.

ARRANGEMENT IN GREY AND BLACK

After dark, he drove us
to the top of the Mountain
and put us out.

We followed a trail through the woods
flashlight beam bouncing off of Spirits.

I keep looking for a narrative,
practicing telling the story in my head.
I keep trying to explain myself in the world.

I am not sure to whom I want to explain this.

I imagined a globe
held on the back of a giant turtle.
I imagined the side of a hill

where I saw him buried under earth.
Seventy acres in California,
mustard fields line the roads.

RELIC

I laid a girl to rest in Ithaca
and dressed myself as a northern beauty.
She settled like a loosened drum

into that ground.
The rattle of nails rang through my pocket
unbraced—no longer in tantrum.

The girl was quiet in the grass
and long as river reeds can grow.
A trap of bones with no ransom.

LEGEND

Sometimes in the telling: a climb
across one's private artifice.

Yarning dark equivalents—
not a stalled car and bus ride back,

but a ghostly moil through stalks
of chronic rain (red road, deep silt).

That's when you picture the Mother of myth—
houndstooth shift, pushbroom—

stooping on the porch, sweeping wrappings
into the dirt. I saw myself finding

a body in the water. I saw myself digging
a pit in the sand.

THE CALICO

I tied twine around the calico's neck
and tried to take her walking.
I want to say it was like
she was taken by a fever—
like a rodeo horse with a sudden
broken back, who after a spiral
of wrenching, falls cold and limp.
My sister found us, cut the cat
loose, wrapped her in a blanket,
I knew about shock
and the voice of a demon living
in both of our throats.

At times I am a choked animal
at others I am the forgiveness
that comes afterward.

OUTBREAK

A small black dog, wicked
in early morning. You're calling
and calling her name. A boat tethered

to shore, rope dragging behind
a truck, a crush of men
outside the warehouse.

This desire of adulthood
and a bottle full of milk.
The Mother left the wire gate

undone. She traveled on wind
like a Viking after gold.
Wet grass. Burnt wood.

A rustle of thinning sheets,
a tangle of stockings—black—
dries on a string in her yard.

ABSOLVED

Night cut you off like a dropped red jar.

The priest pried your eyes,
and your wrinkled look
broke off from the world.

Our murmurs fashion your departure.
Thumbed beads.
In a plush yellow room, your rigor mortis.
Empty as bottles.

A sallow shadow of yours
strapped to the bark of ardor.

All the small hours, your hollow
sinks deeper into bed.

I am twined to your dying—a slow root spreading out of sight.

One epoch more, and I shred the sheets,
moth-anxious and dreary in my dull wrappings.

Your fingers hang fallow as a winter farm.
And now you practice a gradual wilt—
it grates my teeth into jewels.

AFTER A DEATH

Remembering: a body
is a literal thing—
you are vesseled, inland.

I lead the procession
round the mound—ash
box, I swelter. Wondering
how longbones

burn to meagerness
measured by penny pound.
I do not forget your appearance
by the gate—

lengthening out of the copse
a lineament
putting my bottle down.
Between this hill of earth

and yours: a common departure.
I held you just as water turned to fog.

THE INVISIBLE MAN

By the window, on a black bone chair
the germs leave your body through smoke.
Can two tandem blankly
to bash out a cure?
I have read that drones die
in the act of mating.
Honey-stomachs busting
in the rub of it.

The longtime residents
warned me, wind-bitten and slow,
how the storms can peel off
a fishing boat's skin.

By the window, watching men
furl their sails, slick bag balm
along their limbs—turns out
I'm a lasting woman.

From you: blue beads round my neck
a graceless gossamer—
I'll hide within your passing shelter.

RIDING

At the top of the Mountain
fortune holds a cut-down redwood,
me astride it. My head—I'll hide it

from distressed girls who visit me in sleep
and wring their hands,
hurry out from their kitchens to revel
in their own damage.

Birds plummet, sun sinks, rain drops—
things fall out of the sky.
And I'll keep riding for now,
a little ointment on my sores.

STILL LIFE WITH HAND OUTSTRETCHED

I.
Begin in the cold on a patch of earth
pocked with snake holes. Brown boots stand,
little thing in a plaid dress looks on.
Little release as she imagines leaving,
forgetting what's frozen solid.

Inside the ice:
a twittering of bitterness,
an intent to thaw.

II.
As if man could make a better bird
by fusing together a clutch of feathers.

Imitation, variation, subjugation,
not just the end of a tunnel, or a see-you-later.
How can I leave you here battened to the sky?

First, make your eyes the widest they'll go,
thinking you own all of it.
Dear masked shape, dear boxed prize,
I'll tell you what is mine: all of it—
Nothing to wish for but nothing.

SELF-PORTRAIT IN CHAMBER

To see me best, look past

where the rain will prowl

across a particular window,

handle the pane glass

with snake-thick fingerbreadths.

Wing like a warbler, play high-tamer

adding in pluck and ornament.

A symptom in the bracelet—to wrist you

would leash a mourner, make blackout a pet.

Dear grouse, dear regret:

take no mementos, leave no mark.

II. Water

INTO THE DEEPS

Have you still got that plan
for the day age takes your knees
and hollows your chest
along with the rest of a body's nagging arsenals—
to walk into the sea?

A phone call when Bella crawled under the stove
("There goes the last of the cats!") and I'm
not laughing, but coughing.
Let's be done with moving
so much furniture upstairs and down,

transcontinental three times, and once
across the Atlantic. Lifting stirs languor
even in you, bottomless cornfed man.
And in me: side stitch, pang, or
worse—elegiac utterance.

Stomach powders mixed and swallowed,
and still your belly's bloated,
and your ribs swelling into shoals:
let's think of a firmament—
some home for all this machinery.

LEAVINGS

The gate at Forest Hills shuts tightly before blossoms do.
Riding backseat, the window edges down, frees smoke.

Motoring through boneyard boscage, and we
veer toward the water—close enough to lose.

Perhaps it's not that plunge is deep,
but solitude one feels within a freeze.

I want to ripen fast, but have youth in my blood
that bangs against the body.

To recline in a freesia-blue car, and not
crush gently my face flush in woolly sleeves—

it takes all thrust. And when might
my frame be   a machine for reverie?

EXPOSURE

My sleep is out of reach
in the winter—I am this wash of white.

Perhaps inescapably, waiting
for thaw and lake, I scrutinize—

skaters shoe-glide across
each surface keeping the light

un-beached and far off as a darling
held to blurry height. I'm remembering

how each thing has a love
of being near the others,

even a god (who has hated enough)
until his voice is in my throat—

another mistake left tightening.

ISLAND VIEW

He dreams he is expecting.
And I, lying beside him all night

pushing a great boulder up and up
again from sleep's dark valley

dream of tearing one body
out and away from another.

I watch a procession of empty jackets
ferrying themselves across the water to Orcas Island.

Dear, if you find your weakness
for fine weather gives you away,

do something to remind us of your grip.
For instance that delicate cluster

of fingerprints left on a lady's neck,
concealed by a canopy of hair.

Your hold—a ten-gallon gunny-sack
stronger than burlap—please release my eyes.

DEAR ROGUE

His godhead and mine at a red, red tide.
Fireroom's bloom in the morning, a slow, leviathan breach at night.

The angler makes his own light, bioluminescent and fierce.
Dear rogue, you speak like a cloud of black gnats.

So close to these bodies of water,
I open my mouth to listen.

There is a kneeling,
a laying-on of hands,
a rising. Oh.

OPEN BOAT

Not always a cruel ocean,
but a certain unconcern.

I am not inside a violent storm
or hungry animal

but at large, latched
under a dome of glass

that does not care
to show you its colors,

or heal your sick
or stop you from sinking

or feed you the world by hand.
How can I possibly confess

to everything I know,
when there has and always will be

someone sadder, softer, and loftier than me?

WIDE WAVES

You see the bottom of your boat and it's wet.
You are dragging up sea rock in your ever-mended net.
You are pulling yourself to the next stony island.
You've brought crumbles of dead insects, stalks
of cane to tempt the swimmers.
Your eyes bend to the horizon.

Trouble wants purge—collar wants noose
Western skies turn copper, falter.

LULLABY

I am talking about split,
your vacancy.

Nude gloss, body in repose.
These things I am trying to tell you:

the possibility of splinter,
a woman who is overly alert, rapt,

cut through with concave.
A stupid veneer.

Clad in a glass jar.
Fragile bed frame

and a face on the pillow, silent
and marble next to mine.

IN REPOSE

I'm bathing in a dark lake when grey-skinned masses
begin to bubble up around me.

In a fugue, I'm a refugee pulled away
by faceless men as my sister hunts the rocky beach.

You are dragged under the current
while the Father watches and swallows.

At night, I'm always near deep water—
murky and cold as sleep itself.

In my reverie, my mother has gone
silently to her bed.

None of us is safe in rest, pulled under
by the weight of our too-large heads.

It's not tired, this river lapping inside me.
The foggy valley of memory fills with a muddy tide.

BY THE WATER

A figure made of straw grows rot
and falls with the temperature.

Muddy boots by the door
and men blowing leaves from the cusp of the earth.

Brick house, cut knees, how else
can I astonish you?

The gate remains unlocked,
embarrassingly patent, wide.

I'm waiting for your arrival—
a walk on frozen banks.

I was not a rock in that river.
I was not a stone in that stream.

ON THE LAND

A crescendo will occur as you step off the catamaran.

You see two matters of importance
and one of them (a man)
gives the other quick air-punches (a tussle).
But the two turn to hugging and hold the same body.

You want to hold his chest and look
because this is where the water drains,
and you think of a sec-through picture
of a man taking a sip (not an x-ray, but a see-through).

It's a slow realization, really,
that you're not the body,
and the boat's not your boat,
and your mouth is a riot of teeth.

This is when you want to hold his chest
away from you, and take a last look,
after the knowledge that man takes man
and girl takes sip, and water takes boat.

QUESTION

Didn't the dog ruin the flowers,
didn't the stems break, weren't they a symbol

didn't the summer come,
or the nights shorten
to woolly bursts

wasn't the firmament clipped
to make us feel safe—

oscillation and blue heat.
Didn't we stop moving, wasn't the
winter ended a long time ago—

I remember how sky faded clear
in a plastic screen, and wasn't it a symbol
didn't drops fill the street

I don't see your car
through clear drops, banging on the street

didn't I want that rain?

HOUSEWORK

One misspoke by the water,
wallowing. First, I thought

'a spider in the drain,'
then I thought 'a girl

has cut her hair.'
A girl is an orchard

defoliates in the spring.
Fishing for fissure

she discharges me to market.
It might've been nostalgia

bit me, but I still believe
in fallow flesh.

A LAST NOTE

Dear, there's not much more I can do:
the rugs are beaten clean,
my passport's in the mail.

I can follow you with a paper towel
to wipe your traces off each door-knob and spoon.

I've kept your books for you,
and I keep my patience still
in the whirl of a fish tank.

All the plants have died, but
I consider them disposable.

Once this plan was a *pas de deux*
but my dear, I've come down with stomach flu
and a motorcycle rumble.

I've fixed many things here with crazy glue,
but my red cup dropped in the basin.

Soapy knives and forks swim the way sharks do.
A lemon peel floats by, rancid water in my shoes.
I've developed a twitch from the ringing phone.

My dear, I checked the catalogue
and it seems the vine along our siding

why, it's called "The Wandering Jew!"

It ripped the handles off the doors
(I replaced them with bells).

If I want to go outside for a new point of view
I'll have to chew my way through this neat wood frame
but I don't mind teeth marks, do you?

III. Fire

ELEMENTAL

I've been to ten countries
each time looking
for a way to the water.

The world is a burning house
and inside each room—
another way to live on fire.

ADULATION IN A STORM

My proud parts and I come in from the street,
with a pouch of honeycandy to suck. Unpocket

the lot—even a clutch of unraveling wire
(the remains of an erstwhile occasion *de rigueur*).

These mischievous folds won't come undone.
Instead of a long bright cat uncurling before you

I'm somebody's old aunt, laboring out of her dress.
In the dark heat, the sugar's lost shape.

I'm stone to stone with you: cocked in the trappings
of the wood. Undressing, undressing, the faces

of my figure throw their clothes on the floor.
Though I'll see some things not meant for me,

Remember   foul, felled loveliness
how you were adored.

ON DELICACY

Beautiful and bustable,
you're a necessary fixture
in the starting of fire.
A log doesn't burn
without a leaf to light it.

Steam ascends, kettle boiling
to a sharpening pitch. Fathoming
the teacup, feminine and floral
with a chance of fighting it,
of lasting over generations.

These are the moments between the taking
and the having: when windows are closed
but sunlight blares through,
insinuating open air.

This kind of dish does not
yet know the promise of emptiness.

A NEW LANGUAGE

Do you have anything else
to tempt me?

Thin as a young horse,
and dirty in the throat.

I have seen the new dances—
a jangle of parts,

voluminous as the South,
sliding about the room.

I hear talk of a new language—
something more

than a tight blouse
gliding down the avenue.

SHEDDING

The dream was worn.
She had shown

too much of herself—
prone

in fluorescent light.
How will she

peel back her own
catching veneer

as the young doctor,
tremoring

in his newness,
peels the skin

from his cadavers
or the straps of her gown tonight?

APPARITIONS

He dresses in the dark
so as not to wake me
on early mornings, sometimes
three hours before sunrise.

He bends over his coffee
bleary eyes grazing a dim patch
in the likeness of a stranger's
brain plate. He has news to tell.

He slicks his hair back, clips
on cuff links (tiny, gold scorpions
from the antique show) and begins
his black pedal to the hospital.

Other men and women wait
in the dark, unable to dress
and to them he will speak softly
so as not to disturb the dying.

PROVINCIAL PLOT

A ripening leaf brought in from a walk—

I left it on your bookshelf
curling slowly into itself

resting yellowish on Saul Bellow.
Bog-soil harbored on your boots.

Redolence of burn settles on dresses
hanging by the road

where they go through girls like gasoline.
Remember thinning,

reddening on Brewer's heath?
It's the last sunny day—

the watering-can cloyed
in the yard

on the grass. Your hair, thick as thatch,
puts me into a swoon.

WITNESS

Unconditional breathing and a heart
that keeps singing over more and more
American decades. Early spring, raking
rotted leaves, uncovering the body
of a northern bat, perfectly preserved
under dying snowmelt.   I thought

perhaps a resting place in the garbage can
or to be flung in the thicket behind the garage
would provide a proper bridge to beyond.
Rather better for the heart to conceal
a carcass' cooling pith
with a bit of loose dirt

turned over by my spade.
No need to bear much witness past that shade.

POSTCARDS

I.
Deep in falling
I write postcards

to a missing figure.
Life feels

antiquated as we drift
between cafes

cleaving to a bourgeois
concept of life.

II.
The enemy is awake
in my visions.

Swinging across a cracked
and colorful sky,

he is weightless, but tethered
to my bones.

III.
Over decades
we drift through parties

and prayers.
I can be found

near the water,
if you want to know.

IV.
Mother wears a dead dress—
an ex-patriot of the body.

V.
Vents of hot air rise
around him. Pale

in the sun. His hands
look like mine.

Even then, a shadow
of disaster
escapes his frame.

VI.
Upward
velocity

keeps me reaching
on a slant

toward provenance
and the feeling

of old eucalyptus.
I remember it.

We were mud-stuck
and buried.

We are desperate
to never return.

WARMER CLIMES

I was planning to go.

Winter herds of cattle trekked heroically south,
leaving their wrongdoings cliffed into the Mountain.
The day was coming up ripe, bone stuck
in its craw, so it's been—
a warm kingdom for the sort who know the way.

Roadside, a hardness in the jaw,
blood clots at sharp spots,
choring over cracks in the street.
In this heat, no chance of a blossom or a dream of ice.
And though you might ache for "paradise,"
you can throw that dirt to some other dog.

VESTIGES

After I left
solace bloomed and took breaths.

Before: Thanksgiving pies and duck fat,
the hard rind of your boots.

Here is a handle into it, a memory of smoke.
Here is a bird wing fallen from the crow

and more—a book of matches, a book
of prayer. Some days I think of salting,

of wintering, of bracing the windows
and doors. After this life
I will want no more.

VISITANT

There seem to be a few things pressing
against the wall, the shape of a face
rising up, startling the window dressings
and the usual spitting of the furnace.

Victims of chronic splitting feel
something like a tourniquet
about the temple. *Mal à la tête.*
Glass and real flesh
meshed in a sly duet.

Something seems to be coming from
the radio's belly. Another flame gesturing.
I would say of my frame: bowl from
a bitten spoon. More raking over, more stewing.

That rising shape begins to recess—
do you suspect we're bodiless?

WALKING THROUGH FIRE

I'd like to keep what I have, would you?
Crouching so with a wet rag

I hardly know. Little rabbit, I know your look.
Lit by wood flame, you are black with cinder.

At first: flambeau. We burnt books
with bad histories. The driest grass will go,

and though I'm madly for you—
you're nothing next to disaster's glow.

TENDRIL, VENTRICLE

After mania,
I had to remake
myself before

writing back to you.
Dirt under me
began to glow red.

By the time the roots
around my fingers

started spiraling again,
I'd been swaying
to the beat of you

for years. Many girls
know the story
of the unearthly quick line

of narrow ivy,
a vine rising
into the shape

of a killer under cover—
choking out
the tender marrow

from a crab apple
trunk. Siphoning.
When you come back

from the freeze
you remember
with queasiness

the way the cold sits
in your stomach—
a dead egg—

the child that didn't make it.
You are not her.
Remember.

GOODBYE TO ALL THAT

Once you've found hollow
And the hound that's at it, do you see heart—

a barrel of washout blitz still trying to conceive
how fraud apes truth so convincingly?

There is a word for when you're wounded
by those who occupy you.

A girl cut down by greedy hands
and soundless teeth.

Strike the thought: where is my foothold.
This lengthening loves lack—

a sympathy of absences   and assemblies.

IV. Air

LADY SLIPPER

The great thing is having a pit

in the vitals where Spirit won't settle

but reigns all the same. I had a hunger

then lost it. The idea of begging

stretched over me, how breaking a limb

could change a life. I'd offer the eulogy

so solemnly and remember the giant self

that's been in me, and rumored others.

This was before my slight organs grew large,

large enough to give my lack away.

WE ARE THE BIRDS WHO STAYED

Waking inside cold water,
deep fall. Outside, feathers
hit the ground
while winter grows wider.

Still, bark wants burl,
and our down is in tangles.

We've nursed   attractive mistakes,
stuck the harrow, not planned for snow.

Here we go, on a cold, draining river
sure to make remnant of me.

PORTRAIT WITH PATINA

It is in the second version
of our lives

that we have both relented—sorry
to have bitten so

mercilessly at one another's
loose threads.

We are now robust against
each other's virus,

vaccinated, resilient to the foulness
of frenzy and passing rage.

They tell me Earth is bitter
and so is age.

But I wonder what softness
I would have felt

from the doctor as a young man
driving drunk, or hailing

a waitress. And what balm
could I have offered

as a rioting fever, free spinning
around the city in a thrift dress?

Now I find we are hardening
beautifully—

an orange rind to sink
into steeping tea.

THE NATURE CURE

On the way there
I'm mixing a bowl
of shadows in my head.

Applying breathing techniques,
sorting odds and ends of flesh
into buckets

like the estimation of meats
in a can of spam or a sausage.

My pert dog lying in the dusty sun
like an African beetle,

containers filling with rain
and then emptying in the sun.

PORTRAIT ON PERCH

Those first hours atop thrush
were pitted with pear scatter,

ice-bound arms
trailing tin bracelets,

branches groaning,
is this a harvest?

Even a pear tree
grows heavy once a year.

Those first days were resilient
and unaware.

You were turning—
tossed like a handful of hair.

YES, SOME

Some days after you left
and before I rode Greyhound
down the 101,
I found it lying on the sidewalk—
a blackbird wing.

Some things can never be yours.

I have known a clutch of feathers
like grass, bent but not broken, their stems
sprouting like water rapids
where the body would attach.

Some weeks later, flying
above the great mirror of Frisco Bay,
I saw the garbage boats
sharking out to an unseen island,
Glad bags bubbling over,
rapids throwing up the stern.

I didn't forget that beauty extends
in front of you. And then
a sudden crack, loss of sky
or churn of white water.
And sometimes
you can still see the mark—
the tear from the body.

THE LAST WINTER

I want to be done with waiting
and skip ahead to the big thaw I know will come.

I'd like to pack up your plants and my jewels
and drive seven days out

to the long, flat coast where the ocean never freezes
and neighbors pick oranges from each other's trees

in the constant knowledge of summer.
There is nothing I'll miss here

but the fires you built for me
after grey mornings chopping wood in the snow.

THE COLLAPSE

I watched a ripe old man
on that yam-colored bench
at the Waffle House on East Seventh.
He'd begun to rock—

belly bulged to ridges by suspenders.
Trying to stand, he pumped
his feet a while
as if riding a swing, then gave up.

Scraps of my own body
began to melt in the heat,
in the fading, in the not knowing.

We spent some months sleeping
in someone's squat basement
AC turned to high, sinking slowly
into the white sofa—an organ of blankness.

It's called caudal autotomy
when the tail falls off
and the lizard (palsied with lightness)
shoots under a rock.

I saw him alone in that little alcove—
twin vents behind his eyes,
brain-plate throbbing like a heart.
What does it take to rise up?

INTRUDER

A note scrawled on the refrigerator:
Please explain. Are you a memory?

The stranger comes when my familiar is out—
and the yellow sunbeams push but can't pierce
the curtains. I have never seen his face.

But the shape of a winter coat, a whisper of tobacco,
the remnants of a song I haven't heard in so long.

A note scrawled by the bed: Please explain—
Am I a memory? Am I foul?

It must be centuries since I slept on that
broken twin box spring, curled around my sister.

I don't remember how to be a person
who is yet to be found.

RELAPSE

I am amassing an army of self
and now you can't throw me.

An indulgent release, though I wonder
how did I make this cold construction—
wrecked hammer, leathered hide,
holding a slant woman inside?

Blessed, the blockage that thorns you away.
Though, is it coming near the time
now, when you will throw me
a token, even a handkerchief, some
autograph of your affection?

COMING APART

Think of two tender birds
then think of a worm between them.

Juice leaks on the sidewalk:
a fatter worm.

Near my hand, this door.
Near this door, my feet.

Possible worm, impossible bird.
Outside the door, their burying beaks.

PRESERVATION

Oh say *yes*
to embarrassment
and heat.

Accept the ripening
cheeks
and dry

crackling hands
that come from
carrying

something dead.
The frame,
it exits.

And the House,
it stands
much as ever.

Beginning the art
of dissection
with a chicken wing

splitting the skin
as one does at dinner.
Say *yes* to the cleave—

a cut to the bone,
but a clinging too
as man unto wife.

See the beauty of insides.
Play at science
and at understanding,

and go home
with the crisp perfume
of formaldehyde

still on your skin.
God knows where they
arrive at once.

They are the guides
of death, of the body,
of the spider. A beaten path.

ONE OF US

Until now, inventing you
has seemed like a selfish thing to do—
satisfying elemental instincts.

But now I am on the fringe
of understanding

the frantic duty
I have to keep you safe

and boost you into
an unusual flock.

What does our progeny do
but spring up

like emissaries
into the broad open?

AGAINST HAPPINESS

Could I conduct myself
like a woman with a future?

I've been a duck in flight,
hollow-boned, grease dripping
from my frayed and astonished wings.

Someone always on their way
with a shotgun.

In the kitchen, russets on a cutting board.
A bottle of milk added to the pot, whitening the broth.
A scratch on the arm while I swept up the peelings.

The river is grey now, and I study the ceiling,
could almost stoop to praying.
An armful growing cold.

I've been waiting for your arrival—a walk on frozen water.
Winter takes the leaves, and the trees are left kneeling,
bending bare arms in prayer, just penitent enough.

A thousand years later, nursing my progeny
by the glow of a cell phone
still waiting for the sound of gunfire.

WAVING A LONG WHILE

I came back lately from abroad
weighted with botanicals.
I met healthy little girls
with untouched skin and hair.

I bought coffee and raw sugar, colorless
flour in a bowl before the egg—
things that make a life.

Mother, once I laid a trap for you.
Dug a hole, filled it with mud
floated leaves on top,
stood beyond it and called for you
though you didn't come.

In the fairy books, the Mother loses her eyes
in punishment. A finger, the tip of her nose,
teeth fall out of her mouth.
And though I hear this is happening to you,
it wasn't me who spoke the curse out loud.

It's taken me this long to close the gutter,
to take a leaf from your book and burn it.

Wicked visage, shaggy hem of hair, cutting.
Feral thing, hot under the elms, baffling.
Goodbye   you're damp in the heart.

ANTS EATING POISON

Killing is regimental
four to six weeks and I'll do it again.

Each of us
is the knife at someone's throat.

I have been the bully,
I have been waiting

in a bathtub of cooling water.
I have been the young girl

who was unwilling.
I am singing as I execute you—

recalling the black line of swifts
I saw barreling down the sky into a chimney.

Women do this. Gentle women
who coo and soften life's edges for you do this.

I am watching myself
when I feed it to you.

Notes

1. The title, "The Invisible Man" comes from the H.G. Wells novel.
2. The title, "Arrangement in Grey and Black" comes from the James McNeil Whistler painting.
3. The title, "Goodbye to All That" comes from the Joan Didion essay.